LADY RED EGO

Natural Sugars

I0201641

BROKEN SLEEP BOOKS

Published 2020,
Broken Sleep Books:
Cornwall / Wales

brokensleepbooks.com

Second Edition

Lay out your unrest.

Publisher/Editor: Aaron Kent
Editor: Charlie Baylis

Typeset in UK by Aaron Kent

Broken Sleep Books is committed to
a sustainable future for our planet,
and therefore uses print on
demand publication.

brokensleepbooks@gmail.com

ISBN: 978-1-913642-13-6

Contents

Truly, the tree yields bad
fruit.

– Shakespeare,
As You Like it, Act 3 Scene 2

———————————————

For Abbie, who is
still the sweetest.

Natural Sugars

April Hill

Clementine

You like women, yes?
You like to eat them,
squeeze them, smell
their citrus? You like
to peel off their skin in one?

Tooth-rot

Men don't have openings?
What do you mean?
How am I slipping in?
How am I beneath skin?

Masculinity is incomplete.
You cover your entrance
with thin deceit, a hymen ready
to be pierced. Are you not
human, like me? Do you not
have organs, and liquids, and bad dreams?
Do I not have penetrative needs?

Too many sweets
lead to oral decay.
Lady with the lamp,
your feminine inlay.

Harvest

Harvest.
Everything was ripe inside me. The flesh
inside my flesh grew firm and green, and I felt
the bud of it, hard, rubbing between my
limbs everywhere I went. I didn't know how
to garden, only to blossom; it never occurred
to me to take it out.

So Harvest.
I trust you with the insides of me. A warning:
the first bite can be very sour, if only
because it's so fresh. You know I wouldn't lie to you.
You know I only want to give you the best.

Harvesting.
This isn't the love poem I thought I would
write. But this isn't the loving I thought I
would do. I thought it would be all about the
flowers; rather it is all about the fruit. I want
my juice to stain the skin around your lips,
my seeds to get stuck between your teeth.

Harvest – harvesting, harvest time, harvest me.
Dig, dig, digging deep. I have been doing it to myself all
week.
Churning over the rich brown of my mind. My fingers
are stained with soil. They smell of soil. Of
the great insides.

Harvest, harvest, harvesting.
Everything is always cycling in me. I belong to the seasons,
just like everything else earth-grown and natural.
Being with them is natural. I need to stop weather-
checking myself. My body knows what it was made for.

But – harvest time. I woke up smelling like you
because you kissed me last night. I wanted to press myself
into all of your white limbs on show. It's nothing poetic,
but you made me so happy that it kept distracting me from
my own endless
growing pains. Between us, there is something else
green and sun-inclined. Say,
let me sing, hear me sing – this is how I sing!
This is my purpose, produce, present of my soul – say,
my soul! Let me share that with you.

Harvest – Revised

Everything was ripe inside me. Everything was ripe inside me. Everything was ripe inside me. Everything was ripe. Ripe ripe ripe. Inside me.

My soul! My soul! My soul!

Orchard

A quiet sort of farming.
Lines of vitamins,
tied high like baubles,
pregnant and swollen. This
is the art of feeding,
mastered in peaceful
rows. Structure breeds
growth, which all poets
know. A market is only
a temple. You rinse
your hands in a bowl.

Colonnades that grow.
Wood is just soil,
and trunks are fertile torsos.
Their arms branch out,
neurons big enough to watch,
thoughts that want to touch.
Farmer, you keep them apart
like a father searching for
a suitable match. Courtship
favours the individual,
but every tree is a plural
by itself. A brain with
produce. A cacophony
with roots. Lean in.
Listen to all that
ripe, round fruit.

Tongue

raised wet pink
thick lick teeth
pull slick drip
tip lip prod
push delve
rub salt
deep
dip
…
..
.

The Greeting 1

We begin beneath the skin.
Double-headed twin, kinship
that had to be gently
hewed for us to live. You in your
separate existence, your masculine
alternative. I am not a woman.
Sibling, I don't need harmony.

But you found me.
At the tree-line, another brother
holds a baby's head with
untrained delicacy. I understand
that tender skin, the boneless intimacy.
I have been what you will be and your
intuition beats knowledge. Unpolished,
I come to the forest, bringing nothing
but the beginning. It is not a formality.

Penis-envy

Banana-skin,
a Rapunzel prison.
I am waiting,
elbow on window pane,
still half-virgin. You can't see
where I protrude out of tummy,
aching. My tower
grows ever higher. We climb
up our own fantasies, an
elevated reality.
I am only green with
ivy. I am locked in my own
glory. Too big
to feel anything but width.
A circumcised perspective,
my one-eyed prince.
Was it worth the prickly landing?

Leftovers

A rose blossoms into a glass.

It drips. The rose is liquid,
it slips off itself, gives into
gravity. The rose is temporary.
The rose is falling.

I know we do not talk about this.
The rose is not contemporary,
the rose is ancient history, the rose is
your high school memory. The rose is
imaginary, the rose is jelly. It is thick,
and sensitive to movement. The rose
is vibrating. It wants to shake off its body.

So the rose drools, hungry
like any of us,
for new territory. To be beside itself,
to sit next to itself, to look back
and forward with the same gaze.
Cross-eyed rose, how you want to be
funny, how you need the company.
You thought Gertrude made you anew,
she only made you two, made you mirror
yourself like pussy. The glass
is our enemy, each pleat a prison
of familiarity. If I
had written about a crocus, or an iris,
or a lily, you would have some identity.
But you are nothing. You are within the glass;
it is half, you are empty.

Beard

You grew a beard this spring.
Maybe I will too, let the hair close
over my face like a casket. Mask it.
In the black, I thought I felt something
break through my chest, cracking
what was crusted. This violent tenderness,
it began to pour. Each person is
a new sore. This violence,
it began to love itself. Looking back on
its feathered body, it admired its
backside. A violence full of curves
came to me before sleep, and when I
woke I knew I saw you,
or wanted to. Shuttered blindfolds,
but these glass eyes protest and blink.
The black is inside the walls;
you grew a beard this spring.

Lychee

Unholy.
Black out, find out
that black looks blue like a bruise.
Red like a fruit. Wish I could
undo the white flesh that
was bitten out of you. Half-eaten
meal of a woman –
forgive me if I drink at your wounds.

Wish I could
get the red fruit out. De-seeded.
The man hoping I'll bleed something sweet. Want
to squeeze the brown case of his skin
until he pops out like a lychee. A soul is
something you peel,
something you eat. Finger-food
boy delicacy, the thin
hymen-like veil,
a bride,
white skin that I unstick him from
in the surgery that all poetry is.

White-out. There are layers
of teeth, stacked,
like a stadium,
like the arrangement of a grocery:
every buyer is trying to find the
ripest round-thing for the best
price, and every seller is trying to
hide the rotten. Do women soften?
Only when they've been left on display
for too long.

Orgasm is white,
like a lychee.
Betrayal is spiked,

like a lychee.
A crime is something that is done
to numb the wet skin of a
lychee.

A crime is a thief who
reaches in the plastic container
and plucks a fruit like
this is a free country.

It is not a free country.

The Greeting 2

I can't see through the forest.
Trunk thickening twinning a trick
of the light makes me think you
are next to me. I desire nobody.
I am made of lies.
You are made of mischief. Puck
plucks leaves like they are fruit
to eat. His green-stained teeth,
pressed wide, full of smiles.
If I could move, I would walk
the well-worn. As it is,
roots unravel from my feet.

Corn on the Cob

Surely it is time for us
to stop talking about it
and just skewer each other
on sticks.

Labour

I pry love from between
conkers when the skin
is still green. I put up with
being spiked on every pad
of my fingers. I pull like I
am undressing sweetcorn
in great papery strips.
I suck on love like I am
trying to loosen its grip.
My breath dips. Push back
cuticle and cut nail for this.
Avoid men and revenge and
acrylic

       just to be near you.
Nothing is close enough.
I gnaw on the bones.
I stew until the meat falls.
I eat the brain and eyes
and nose. I never say no.
I never say go. I hammer
into love like brick tea and
boil until it softens,
a willing body beneath me.

Love
is like pulling teeth or
surgery. The metallic,
fleshy remembering.
The bright lights
and patience. Terrifying
and transformative
and necessary.

Abbie-Apple

Even though
my lips swell,
two fat animals
of irritation,
angry and natural
dermal. Even though
my gums itch,
pulling red over
my teeth. Even
though I can't see –
the sugar is worth the allergy.
This apple of Abbie,
dangling like forbidden
knowledge. If he did
not want you bitten, why
hang you in reach?

Pink lady, your striped
skin stings. Tears,
a membrane giving in.
I am the insect, unable to resist.
Drawn by some deep instinct.
Death as an act of worship.
The flesh, the flesh, the flesh.
Born to repeat. Sacrificially sweet.

The Greeting 3

You don't have to coax me.
You don't have to tempt me in.

When I came here, I was only a girl
and being a girl is almost like being nothing.
My slender invisibility, my whole-body-valve,
thrumming with someone else's liquid beat.
Blood eventually wears away meat, lapping
at skin like an affectionate dog. Everyone
becomes a man around me, and being a man
is almost like being a god. Bearded, floating,
always in periphery. I don't need to climb the sky
to reach him. I just need to stop praying.

And was girlhood such a bad thing? So close
to my mother and father it was like I was
wearing their clothes, shaving my chin,
pushing in hooked earrings mindlessly.
I remember sleeping between them,
all eyes and half-height, staring up at the ceiling.
Later, people came into my bed
who made night into warm, green forests.

Acknowledgements

Firstly, thank you to Aaron Kent and Charlie Baylis for taking on this body of work. As always, thank you to Queer Words Project Scotland and Rachel Plummer for bringing me into the published world of poetry.

I'm grateful to all the queer poets who came before me and were so formative in my readings. Their work gave me a language for my desires.

In a similar vein, I want to thank all my friends who have come to readings and bought pamphlets and magazines and books to show their support – it's always so deeply appreciated. But I especially want to thank my queer friends, because I wouldn't be where I am without you.

And finally, of course thank you to my parents, and to Abbie.

LAY OUT YOUR UNREST

www.ingramcontent.com/pod-product-compliance
Lightning Source LLC
Chambersburg PA
CBHW071942020426
42331CB00010B/2984